THE FIVE CLOCKS

MARTIN JOOS

THE FIVE CLOCKS

With an Introduction by
Albert H. Marckwardt

A HARVEST/HBJ BOOK
HARCOURT BRACE JOVANOVICH
NEW YORK AND LONDON

CONTENTS

INTRODUCTION

I T has taken a long time for linguistic scholarship to recognize the complex ways in which every speaker adjusts his language to the various contexts in which he employs it. It has taken even longer to develop a mechanism for describing in specific and systematic terms the nature of these linguistic adjustments. The present work is really the first to have undertaken this task with respect to the English language. This is one set of faces of the five clocks, and in order to appreciate their significance, we must see them in the light of the mechanisms that preceded them.

During much of the nineteenth century and even part of the twentieth, especially in books written for the general public, judgments on the English language were presented in terms of a simple dichotomy. Words and expressions were either right or wrong, correct or incorrect. Decisions about them were generally based upon tradition or analogy.

There followed a period when writers on the English language treated the range of usage in terms of a ladder-like series of levels. The basic or minimal form of the ladder consisted of three steps: Formal or Literary English at the top; a middle stage characterized as Informal or Colloquial; a bottom rung stigmatized as Vulgar or Illiterate. This was expanded at times, usually by recognizing distinctions in the middle range (Formal Colloquial, Low Colloquial) or by inserting Slang or Dialect as additional levels in this strangely assorted series. Today it is easy to be superior about these early efforts, but they did arise from an honest effort to break away from an oversimplified view of language as all black or all white.

The first major attack upon the single hierarchy of language levels came in 1947, when Professor John Kenyon of Hiram College addressed the College English Group of Northeastern Ohio. His paper was subsequently published in the journal *College English,* under the title "Cultural Levels and Functional Varieties of English." The title itself suggests Kenyon's thesis, namely that the single hierarchical arrangement of language levels was, in effect, "a false combination of two distinct and incommensurable categories." Kenyon recognized standard and substandard as cultural levels, familiar and formal as functional varieties of language. This made it possible for him to assign a status of respectability to the familiar or informal speech and writing of cultivated and educated users of the language rather than to condemn it to an inferior position on the traditional ladder.

Kenyon blamed himself, along with others, for having perpetuated the earlier confusion of level and variety, and modestly concluded that he scarcely dared hope for much change or reform in subsequent treatments of the levels of English. Actually his work did have considerable effect. The more enlightened textbook writers began to treat the concept *colloquial* somewhat more gently, and at times the ladder-like diagrams were replaced by interlocking circles, placed horizontally rather than vertically.

Even so, Kenyon's treatment left much to be desired, especially in that it again settled for simple dichotomies. The social and educational structure of our society is too complex, too much of a continuum for its language to be adequately classified by one seal of approval (Standard) and one label of disapproval (Substandard). Likewise, the situations in which we communicate have in them too many variables, too many degrees of familiarity or formality to permit a satisfactory grouping into just two categories. It is in connection with this latter point that the present work makes a significant contribution.

It is interesting to note that Professor Joos's first discussion of the five styles of English is to be found in his monograph *English Language and Linguistics,* written in the autumn of 1958 for students and teachers of English in Yugoslavia. In a section entitled "The Language in Its Social Matrix," he began with the observation that both British and American English differed from a pattern common among the European languages, "in which formality continues longer among strangers of higher rank and education." "A learner of English," he pointed out, "has the task of reversing his correlation between prestige and formality."

Despite its Balkan unveiling, the incident

that crystallized this analysis of the styles of English had occurred at the University of Alberta in the summer of 1958, where Professor Joos offered a course in Modern English Grammar. His class there consisted of thirty-eight teachers of English, most of them with long experience. As an introductory device, he had asked this group to evaluate two paragraphs of written prose. As he describes it, "Most of them tore into it with gusto and proved that it was the work of a backward teen-ager, messily constructed and full of slang and grammatical errors." Actually the selection had been taken from *The Cherokee Strip* by Marquis James, winner of two Pulitzer Prizes for his writing.

The shock of the disclosure led to a situation where Joos and his class could examine the sounds and grammatical forms of English objectively, and ultimately they arrived at a point where stylistics had to be taken into consideration in order to explain choices from among forms that were grammatically equivalent. As Joos has written, "Now I had long known that I had close to half a dozen styles of English myself, and certainly more than three; offhand, then, I told them that I thought there were five styles and suggested that we might operate as a seminar for a while to nail them down properly."

From a purely technical and descriptive point of view, the value of *The Five Clocks* lies in its helpful classification and accurate description of the situations in which we communicate, and in connecting each of these with certain linguistic features characteristic of the style of discourse. For example, the casual style is for friends, acquaintances, insiders. There is an absence of background information and no reliance on listeners' participation. The linguistic devices connected with it are ellipsis and slang. Analogous treatment is given to the entire range of styles, from intimate to frozen. Much more could be done with respect to each of the styles, but this marks out an approach and charts the way.

There is more here, however, than merely a tool for the analysis of speech and writing, valuable as this is. The book is designed to overcome what the author calls the English-usage guilt-feelings of the normal American. For this reason the reader is introduced, not just to one, but to four usage dimensions of native central English: age, breadth, and responsibility, as well as style. And this, of course, is what the author meant when in the earlier version he spoke of the language in its social matrix. Sociolinguistics has recently become a fashionable field of research. What we must recognize about it is that it is by no means limited to problems of multilingualism, social dialect, and language standardization. Its first concern lies behind social engineering and language planning and must necessarily deal with the complex relationships between language and the specific social environments.

It was suggested earlier that the five clocks had more than a single face. Thus far our attention has been concentrated entirely upon the value of this work as a treatment of stylistics. But the author has remarked, "My fan-letters have all been from women, who treat it as a literary work, which is the way it was meant to be treated. Published use of it has all been by men, and they gravely come to terms with the technical information without even mentioning its last chapter."

Actually the literary purpose is apparent throughout the work; it is only in the last chapter that it has taken over completely. Toward the end of the work the author explains that there are two sects of humans, one of which plays with literature, the other with science. "They have got to get together to propagate the community of the future."

Although Joos mentions Shaw, Goethe, and Wolfram and ignores Ovid, what he has written is one of the *Metamorphoses*. He begins with Miss Fidditch, a character originally named by Henry Lee Smith, Jr., in one of his more devastating moments but described by H. L. Mencken two decades earlier as one of the old-maid schoolteachers who would rather parse than eat. As she is described here, "Webster is one Webster, and Miss Fidditch is his prophet." At the end she emerges as Candida, and if she has not quite acquired the divine insight of her prototype, she has begun to distinguish between reality on the one hand and follies, illusions, and vanity on the other. According to Joos, there is a writer inside of her, struggling to break out of the chrysalis. But inside of the writer there is the person, and it is the emergence of the person that fascinates.

The change is gradual. At the outset, Miss Fidditch hovering in the wings serves principally as an off-stage presence, clucking in outrage at the author's sallies against linguistic folklore. At this point his comments to her are brief, designed to annihilate. As the discussion proceeds to a concern with literature and the frozen style, her comments lengthen. She becomes engaged in the discussion—monologue slowly becomes dialogue, and when she recognizes in the author's definition of classical text a similarity to the five clocks, she is addressed as Candida for the first time.

Sinners do not repent overnight, nor is the transformation of Miss Fidditch achieved without backsliding. She regresses from time to time, but by the end of Chapter V the author has called her Candy at least once and she has it made. The last chapter belongs completely to her, even though she still lapses into Miss Frankenstein on one occasion.

Nevertheless, carried away though we may be by the story detail, we must not overlook the force at work, namely the power of looking at language and seeing it whole, for that is still what the book is primarily about. It is thinking and learning about language, not only as a human instrument but as an instrument of humanity that is responsible for the metamorphosis of Miss Fidditch. Here is the message and the hope for those of us who are professionally dedicated to the study of language. To paraphrase a recent speech by William Arrowsmith, in *The Five Clocks* we can find a visible embodiment of the realized humanity of our skill, scholarship, intelligence, and aspiration.

ALBERT H. MARCKWARDT
Princeton University

Ballyhough railway station has two clocks which disagree by some six minutes. When one helpful Englishman pointed the fact out to a porter, his reply was 'Faith, sir, if they was to tell the same time, why would we be having two of them?'

THE FIVE CLOCKS

I

TOO MANY CLOCKS

THAT more than one kind of English is likely to be in use at the same time and place is a notorious fact. So is sex, for that matter, or the weather. But our accommodations to those facts are not equally realistic. We have easily understood that evolution has so shaped our planet's flora and fauna that agriculture is best served by fluctuating weather and cyclical seasons. With a great deal more effort, we are coming to understand that sex is here to stay and may even have a sort of survival-value— that its seasons and its vagaries may conceivably be essential to the business of being human.

Long ago taught to give weather its highest praise by calling it 'seasonable,' we have been learning recently to treat sex with the same

3

respect for facts. The intellectual gain is great, however few may value it. Much greater, some say, is the profit that comes from not sending children into adulthood with useless burdens of guilt.

English-usage guilt-feelings have not yet been noticeably eased by the work of linguistic scientists, parallel to the work done by the psychiatrists. It is still our custom unhesitatingly and unthinkingly to demand that the clocks of language all be set to Central Standard Time. And each normal American is taught thoroughly, if not to keep accurate time, at least to feel ashamed whenever he notices that a clock of his is out of step with the English Department's tower-clock. Naturally he avoids looking aloft when he can. Then his linguistic guilt hides deep in his subconscious mind and there secretly gnaws away at the underpinnings of his public personality. Freud or Kinsey may have strengthened his private self-respect, but in his social life he is still in uneasy bondage to the gospel according to Webster as expounded by Miss Fidditch.

Shall the porter speak up? Well, it isn't likely to do much good this year. But the porter is a sort of Court Fool and won't lose his job for speaking up once. And if enough of us speak up, travelers may learn to read clocks with more sympathy and self-respect.

The Ballyhough situation was simple. But English, like national languages in general, has five clocks. And the times that they tell are not simply earlier and later; they differ sidewise too, and in several directions. Naturally. A community has a complex structure, with variously differing needs and occasions. How could it scrape along with only one pattern of English usage? (Webster, of course! — Well, . . .)

It would be very little better served with a single range of usages, differing along the length of a single scale. And yet our public theory of English is all laid out along just such a single yardstick. (Webster is one Webster, and Miss Fidditch is his prophet.)

We have not yet learned to speak of English as we speak of the weather and agriculture, and as we are slowly learning to speak of sex and survival. In the school folklore called 'grammar' for lack of effective challenge—a sort of numerology taught in high-schools instead of algebra, an astrology masquerading as astronomy in our colleges—we are bound to speak of English usage only in a simplistic way, like a proper Victorian maiden lady speaking of Men.

Ask a normal citizen to compare 'if they was to tell the same time' with 'if they were to tell the same time' and he will check by Miss Fidditch's tape: 'Bad, fair, good, better, best = Correct.' And that's about all. Oh yes; he will deplore the conditions which prevail, he will mutter that he too has sinned and fallen short of Webster, and he will be worried about his son's English. Then he will wander off into spelling-reform and Communism.

But now if you press him for a program, he will suggest installing a master-clock system. He will promise to speak up in the next P.T.A. meeting for more and better grammar teaching, like they had in Webster's day. What he doesn't know is that he himself has two English-usage clocks as adequately adjusted as any railroad-man's watch, for use on different occasions, plus three others that are more or less reliable depending on his experiences and the distances to his horizons. And he will be baffled by your lunacy if you casually say what linguists know: That he built and adjusted those clocks himself, with less help than hindrance from schooling.

What he does know is that his usage varies, as he thinks. The fact is that his several usages do not vary enough to matter, any one

6

of them. They alternate with each other, like his pajamas and overalls and committee-meeting suit, each tailored so as not to bind and so that he finds the pockets without looking. And he has one master-clock to tell him when to change. (Tsk, tsk! Mixed metaphor! — Pray for me, Miss F.)

Then, when he happens to notice that the garments differ, he parrots her appraisals of better and worse. Finally he pleads 'No contest,' on the theory that he was surely wrong every time—that correctness is for teachers, who have the word from Webster. (Where did Webster get it from? — Excuse me, I'm busy.)

Bad, fair, good, better, best. Only the best is Correct. No busy man can be Correct. But his wife can. That's what women are for. That's why we have women to teach English and type our letters and go to church for us and discover for us that the English say 'Aren't I?' while we sinfully hunt golf balls in the rough on Sunday, and, when our partner finds two of them, ask 'which is me?' (Webster: colloq. — Professor K of Harvard: I speak colloq myself, and sometimes I write it.)

Only the porter . . . Only a few of us today are aware of the other scales of English usage. It is our business to consciously know about their social utility. We have to say 'consciously,' for, beneath their cant, the members of the community are unconsciously familiar with those other values: that is, in fact, what it means to 'be a member of' a community. The unaware familiarity is what makes the values effective and gives the individual his profit from them. The kids know that; that's why they don't listen to Miss Fidditch — they have their eye on the main chance. (Where does it say how to sweet-talk in French? — Who cares! She's [He's] American.)

Must usages differ? We might as well ask whether quadrupeds must have four legs and snakes have none. Each question is meaningful —to a believer in Original Sin. A scout from Mars would ask no such questions. He would take each usage as belonging to a current stage in a continuing evolution. And he would not confuse his research with a Golden-Age myth or a Progress theory—nor with a World-is-going-to-the-dogs fallacy either.

His basic research assumption would be: Since usage differences call for efforts to keep them under control, there must be rewards for the efforts. They must have survival-values. Then he would set about tabulating differences,

8

efforts, and values. Rather soon, he would examine how the young advance toward better control and improved chances of survival. Example: 'Hi, Toots!' — 'Don't be such a goof!' (Quiet there, Miss F. These are people preparing for examinations.)

Efforts and values are never perfectly in equilibrium. That is why usages change: they are constantly being readjusted to make up for the constant erosion that washes out the profits. In one word, a classical instance of homeostasis —a term which our scout learned at home on Mars from medical research and found useful in describing his native culture. Catabolism and metabolism. When you assume a fixed position, you're dead. Dead as Caesar or a Siberian mammoth. Or Webster.

When too many people had abandoned 'Ain't I?' we promptly used the tar-brush on 'Pleased to meet you.' To a social animal, the question of first importance always is 'What group am I in?' The second question is 'How do I stand within the group?' Only third are the message transactions, namely 'How are things changing within my group?' A poor fourth is 'How's the weather?'—matters of information. Fifth (earlier only for pedants) is

9

'How does my group rank among other groups?'—with respect to language usage, this is 'correctness.'

Among other things—among a great many others!—the scout from Mars must examine the match-up between the bad-to-best scale of English usage and the parallel scales of occasions, of moods, and of men. It would be foolish to assume in advance that they are just bad-to-best men. (You mean that the Good Guys don't always flaunt Webster and the Bad Guys don't always flout Webster? — Precisely.)

Our scout's report would contain a footnote pointing out that 'bad' is a word also used for an inedible egg, and that 'bad egg' is a personal epithet; also that 'the best butter' occurs in the literature. His chapter on the bad-to-best scale could be a fascinating one. But we have no right to assume that it would be the longest chapter, or the most important one in the scout's view. By trying hard to be as objective as a man from Mars, let's see how close we can come to reconstructing his report.

And Webster? — Complete in his Appendix. But we don't need to reprint it because it's in the Museum of Natural History. Or we could ask Miss Fidditch. We probably will anyhow.

II

HOW MANY CLOCKS?

Here are, in order of importance, four of the usage-scales of native central English:

AGE	STYLE	BREADTH	RESPONSIBILITY
senile	frozen	genteel	best
mature	formal	puristic	better
teenage	consultative	standard	good
child	casual	provincial	fair
baby	intimate	popular	bad

These four scales are essentially independent; relations among them are not identities. (But isn't the best English genteel? — That must be Miss Fidditch talking.)

AGE: The frame within which all other scales develop. Though this is the most important of them all, we shall have very little to say about the age-scale of usage because nothing can be done about it directly, and that little will have to wait to near the end.

11

STYLE: Here are the five clocks to which we shall principally devote our attention. They may be called 'higher' and 'lower' for convenience in referring to the tabulation; but that doesn't mean anything like relative superiority. More later.

BREADTH: This scale measures breadth of experience and of self-limitation. From popular English up to standard English, your experiences broaden your usages; and from there up to genteel you narrow them again to suit your personality. Nothing further.

RESPONSIBILITY: Here at last is the actual usage-scale nearest to Miss Fidditch's mythical scale of excellence, and we borrow her scale-labels but not her meanings for them, eliminating her favorite synonym 'correct' for the top. More immediately.

Much as linguists hate to admit it, the responsibility scale does exist. It even has considerable though minor importance. Its importance is minor because we use it only in forming social clusters, momentary or lasting. If we have done a good job, the cluster is homogeneous on the responsibility scale, which holds it together as a social group. Then we can forget the responsibility-ratings of the group's members, because we are done using them: they are used only in first forming the group or in adding or dropping members. This responsibility scale needs to be cleared out of the way, to prevent confusion, before we consider the five clocks of style.

The reason why linguists dislike acknowledging the responsibility scale is that any acknowledgment of its existence is customarily taken as an endorsement of the 'quality' theory of usage which they of course reject. That quality theory holds that usages are intrinsically good or bad—that each usage is by itself absolutely good or absolutely bad, under a taboo-rule, without inquiring into what good or evil it performs in real life. For example, 'ain't' and 'hisself' are rated as bad English (or 'not English' to make the condemnation stronger by including a self-contradiction in it); and every essay at discussing their badness counts as an attempt to introduce poison into the water-supply. (What does Webster say? Well, that settles it, doesn't it? I don't see what good it would do to discuss the matter any further.)

Now those linguists are right to a certain extent. 'Ain't I?' has just as respectable an origin as 'Aren't we?'—and, ultimately, a more respectable origin than 'Aren't I?' as it is pronounced by most of those Americans who use

it. Again, in view of everybody's 'myself, our-
selves, yourself, yourselves' the bad minority's
'hisself, theirselves' would be more grammatical if logic governed grammar. Yet the origin
and the logic don't matter; here the master rule
has been known for centuries: Treason doth
never prosper; what's the reason? Why, if it
prosper, none dare call it treason. In short, the
community's choice of what shall count as the
norm and what shall be rated as 'bad' (in general, even by those who use it) apparently is an
arbitrary choice, so that usage is never good or
bad but thinking makes it so.

What, never? There is more to it than that.
There is something about social living that cre-
ates a responsibility-scale of usage; and when
we have examined the natural basis of that
scale, we shall see why the folklore calls it a
quality scale.

The community's survival depends on cooperation; and adequate cooperation depends
on recognizing the more and the less responsible types of persons around us. We need to
identify the natural burden-bearers of the community so that we can give them the responsibility which is heaviest of all: we make
them responsible for cooperation itself. Then
the majority of us can function carefree in our

square and round niches, free of the burden of maintaining the cooperation-net which joins us all. Some few of us have a strong interest in cooperation-nets without much competence in them; we are placed as letter-carriers and writers and legislators and teachers and so on; and for those jobs we are selected by tests which discriminate between interest and talent in the maintenance of cooperation.

In any case, the community places us principally by language-use tests which measure us on the various usage scales. Conversely, each of us selects others. For the present, we are interested in just one scale, namely responsibility—a personality scale and a usage scale running quite accurately parallel to each other.

We start very early learning to use this scale. It would be an exceptionally foolish ten-year-old who trusted a well-groomed sharper in preference to a judge in a bathing-suit. And he selects the more responsible person principally by listening, for the same reason that an employer wants an interview with each job-seeker—an interview for which no handbook is needed, for the oral code is public property.

The oral code for responsible personalities is indeed in part arbitrary, conventional: 'himself,' not 'hisself.' But the convention has a natural base, and in a very simple way. Responsible language does not palter. It is explicit. It commits the speaker. The responsible speaker is under a sort of almost morbid compulsion to leave himself no way out of his commitment. The responsibility-dialect does not mumble; its grammar does not contradict itself; its semantics doesn't weasel. That is its basis; 'himself' and the rest are conventional, but they borrow their strength from the natural basis; they are overlays, but the basis is strong enough to overpower the illogicality of 'himself.'

Miss Fidditch's shibboleths are about half conventional overlays. Did she create them? No; the community did, on the theory that birds of a feather flock together. Through some historical accident—some random fluctuation in the distribution of 'himself' and 'hisself' among members of the community—it happened that 'himself' came to be regarded as relatively more common in the responsibility-dialect. It may not have been actually more common there, but the community at large at least thought it was, and that was enough. Flocking did the rest. Those young people who aspired to responsibilities (perhaps only subconsciously aspired) selected 'himself' (normally without awareness of what they were doing or why), while those who aspired to irresponsible lives selected 'hisself' if it was conventionally available to them.

If it was not, they instead selected effete usages. Vulgarity and effeteness use equivalent signals in our culture. Each supplies its fellowship with passwords. For the community at large, the passwords are signals saying 'No responsibilities wanted!' And we take them at their word—for this part of our communication-system—the more certainly because the whole code works subconsciously.

Miss Fidditch's mistake is in trying to work out the code consciously and logically, instead of simply listening to what clearly responsible people actually say. Sometimes, however, she does listen; and then if she tries to teach what she has learned, and if her more responsible pupils learn to speak that way, Miss Fidditch is apt to imagine that her teaching is what taught them. That is an illusion. Responsibility earns respect; therefore most people (not all!) try for a step higher on the responsibility scale of English usage: simply to earn the respect of others, even irresponsible persons will try this if they don't feel the danger in it. In any case, that is why usages once labeled 'bad' always dwindle and ultimately vanish. Not because

Miss Fidditch banned them! The kids aren't listening to her; they listen to Uncle David who is an aviator and to Dr. Henderson, perhaps also to historical and fictional characters if the school is doing its proper job. Miss Fidditch is convinced that bad English is gaining ground; she is only looking for burglars under the bed; statistics says the opposite, item by item. (Don't cry, Miss Fidditch! Homeostasis will keep up your supply of bad English, never fear!)

Finally, the community prefers the center of the scale: 'good' usage, not 'best.' It routinely rejects morbidly honest candidates for office, and the best English counts as the disqualification that makes a teacher.

III

INFORMAL CLOCKS

Now for the Five Clocks that will concern us for the rest of this occasion—the five styles duly tabulated on page 11. With a single exception, there is no law requiring a speaker to confine himself to a single style for one occasion; in general, he is free to shift to another style, perhaps even within the sentence. But normally only two neighboring styles are used alternately, and it is anti-social to shift two or more steps in a single jump, for instance from casual to formal. When the five styles have been separately and comparatively described, the details of shifting will be obvious.

We begin with 'good standard mature consultative style' because the readers of this report are presumably best at home there. The community itself, though its average age is in the 'mature' bracket, is best at home in the completely central 'good standard teenage consultative style,' used for replanning baseball and other matters of moment. To add to the confusion, your reporter is writing good standard mature formal style, with many borrowings from the consultative and casual styles, plus shreds and patches of frozen style placed with honest care.

On the next page there is a long sample of good standard mature consultative style. We know that it is genuine: it was recorded from a telephone line. Here it is copied from *The Structure of English,* by Charles Carpenter Fries, with fictitious names used for smoothness instead of giving only initials as in the book. One speaker's words are italicized. Quoting Fries: 'These oral reactions on the hearer's part do not interfere with the continuous flow of utterances of the speaker. They simply serve to give something of the hearer's reaction and to signal the fact that he is listening attentively to the speaker.'[1] In face-to-face consultation, some of these may be silent, consisting of nods and smiles and the like; but it is clear that the audible ones were not invented recently for

[1] Charles Carpenter Fries, *The Structure of English* (New York: Harcourt, Brace & World, 1952), p. 50.

telephone use, since they can all be documented from earlier printed books. In a lively conversation the total number of listener's insertions, audible and silent together, is likely to be much greater than what we find here, and the audible ones alone perhaps roughly as many as here, that is to say about one every six seconds.

I wanted to tell you one more thing I've been
2 talking with Mr. Davis in the purchasing department about our typewriters *yes* that order
4 went in March seventh however it seems that we are about eighth on the list *I see* we were
6 up about three but it seems that for that type of typewriter we're about eighth that's for a
8 fourteen-inch carriage with pica type *I see* now he told me that Royce's have in stock the
10 fourteen-inch carriage typewriters with elite type *oh* and elite type varies sometimes it's
12 quite small and sometimes it's almost as large as pica *yes I know* he suggested that we go
14 down and get Mrs. Royce and tell her who we are and that he sent us and try the fourteen-
16 inch typewriters and see if our stencils would work with such type *I see* and if we can use
18 them to get them right away because they have those in stock and we won't have to wait *that's*
20 *right* we're short one typewriter right now as far as having adequate facilities for the staff
22 is concerned *yes* we're short and we want to

get rid of those rentals *that's right* but they are
24 expecting within two weeks or so to be receiving—ah—to start receiving their orders on
26 eleven-inch machines with pica type *oh* and of
course pica type has always been best for our
28 stencils *yes* but I rather think there might be
a chance that we can work with elite type *well*
30 *you go over and try them and see what they're*
like and do that as soon as you can so that
32 *we'll not miss our chance at these*[2]

Consultative style is the easiest kind of English to describe, though that doesn't matter so
much because we're not going to write its grammar here. Still, a few remarks may not be
amiss. We see that 'we won't' [19] and 'we'll
not' [32] are not synonymous: in the latter,
'will' is not negated but only the following
words are, so that the message is 'we'll surely
get our chance at these.' We can see that 'oh'
[11, 26] acknowledges receipt of new information, 'I see' [5, 8, 17] certifies that it has been
understood, 'yes' [3, 22, 28] approves the
other's understanding of the situation, and
'that's right' [19-20, 23] approves the other's de-
cision. Such differences in meanings are so important in consultation that even face to face
the listener's contributions will not remain
entirely silent.

[2] *Ibid.,* p. 51.

The two defining features of consultative style are: (1) The speaker supplies background information—he does not assume that he will be understood without it—such information as 'elite type varies' [11]. (2) The addressee participates continuously. Because of these two features, consultative style is our norm for coming to terms with strangers—people who speak our language but whose personal stock of information may be different.

But treating the listener as a stranger is hard work in the long run; therefore we sooner or later try to form a social group with him. Our most powerful device for accomplishing this is the use of casual style. Casual style is for friends, acquaintances, insiders; addressed to a stranger, it serves to make him an insider simply by treating him as an insider. Negatively, there is absence of background information and no reliance on listeners' participation. This is not rudeness; it pays the addressee the compliment of supposing that he will understand without those aids. On the positive side, we have two devices which do the same job directly: (1) ellipsis, and (2) slang, the two defining features of casual style.

The term 'slang' is used here in a strict sense, not in the loose popular sense which makes it a term of condemnation for anything and everything in language which is discountenanced: substandard usage, dialect, cant, jargon, or merely slovenliness. A dictionary definition (in Webster's New International Second Edition) includes 'cant' as one meaning of 'slang' and 'jargon' as a second, both of which we eliminate; the third meaning there is what we will follow: 'Language comprising certain widely current but usually ephemeral terms (especially coined or clipped words, or words used in special senses, or phrases, usually metaphors or similes) having a forced, fantastic, or grotesque meaning, or exhibiting eccentric or extravagant humor or fancy.' Examples: 'leather' is not slang but thieves' cant for 'wallet;' 'to be with it' is not slang but carny jargon; 'to be in the know' was slang in the sixteenth century but is now standard English; 'skiddoo' is dead slang; it is useless to quote live slang, because it is pretty certain to be dead before this page is read.

The purpose of ellipsis and the purpose of slang is the same; but they are opposite in their description and opposite in their history. Ellipsis is a minus feature and is very stable historically; slang is a plus feature and is absolutely unstable. Yet both signify the same: that the ad-

24

dressee, an insider, will understand what not everybody would be able to decipher.

Ellipsis (omission) makes most of the difference between casual grammar and consultative grammar. 'I believe that I can find one' is proper (though not required) in consultative grammar, but casual English requires a shorter form, say 'I believe I can find one' if not the still more elliptical 'Believe I can find one.' All the weak words of English can be omitted at the beginning of a casual sentence: 'Been a good thing if . . .' for 'It would have been a good thing if . . .' and similarly [A] friend of mine . . .' or '[The] coffee's cold.' Some ellipsis is only phonological: 'Can I help you?' is consultative and 'C'n I help you?' is casual. Modern 'cute' from original 'acute' and 'fence' from 'defence' are two out of many words which originated in casual style and have since been promoted; similarly, 'Thank you' from 'I thank you' has been promoted all the way to formal style, while 'Thanks' from 'Many thanks' or 'Much thanks' (Shakespeare) has been promoted only to consultative. Aside from such little shifts in the tradition, ellipsis is stable: the elliptical expressions in use today can nearly all be found in Shakespeare, for instance 'Thanks.'

As an institution, slang is also ancient; but each individual slang expression is, on the contrary, necessarily unstable. The reason is obvious. Because the utility of any slang expression for classing the addressee as an insider (or excluding an unwanted listener as an outsider) depends on the fact—or at least the polite fiction—that only a minority of the population understands this bit of slang, each slang expression is necessarily ephemeral; for when that fiction has become transparent with age, its purpose is foiled, and then the useless slang is abandoned while new slang has to be created to take its place—not new slang of the same meaning, of course, but just enough new slang to maintain a normal supply. The abandoned slang is then 'dead slang,' a few items of which may still be resurrected as period-pieces for jocular or nostalgic employment, for instance 'kiddo' or 'for crying out loud.' (How awful! — That's life, Miss Fidditch.)

It's what is called 'half-life' in nuclear physics. The half-life of a slang expression is of the order of magnitude of one year, which implies that about one specimen in a thousand will survive for ten years, and thus become tough enough to last indefinitely; example: 'to be in the know.' When slang is created for use in literature, the slang is dignified by such titles as 'trope, simile, metaphor,' — and it is routinely rejected when outworn there also. (I can't believe it. — You don't have to, Miss F.)

Besides these two pattern devices—ellipsis and slang—casual style is marked by an arbitrary list of formulas, all very stable, which are learned individually and used to identify the style for the hearer's convenience. 'Come on!' has been one of these identifiers since before the time of Shakespeare (*The Tempest*, I, ii, 308); and all this while, every adult native speaker of English to whom it was addressed has unconsciously known that the speaker was using casual style and has reacted accordingly —and the speaker, without knowing why he did it, has used it to procure that reaction. It is all automatic, unconscious, just as the speaker of a falsehood is not aware that his motive for saying 'as a matter of fact' is to label it as false—a Freudian confession which is institutional in English. (I'm sure I never . . . — I believe you!)

Each style has its own list of such conventional formulas, which we may call 'code-labels' because they serve both to carry part of the message and to identify the style. The identifying function of a code-label is uniformly effective; its message-bearing function varies freely from nothing at all to a full message-fraction. Thus 'Come on!' means anything from 'Consider yourself among friends' to 'You're invited'; while 'Come on, cheer up!' means nothing but 'Cheer up because you're among friends.' There is of course a long list of casual code-labels, but 'Come on!' is one of the commonest.

Consultative code-labels include the standard list of listener's insertions 'yes [professorial for *yeah*], yeah, unhunh, that's right, oh, I see, yes I know' and a very few others, plus the 'well' that is used to reverse the rôles between listener and speaker. Another class of consultative code-labels consists of formulas for meeting that fluency problem which casual style evades by never tackling totally new topics; these are skeleton-keys for opening new doors without fumbling for the exact key which formal style will seek out at leisure. In our sample [page 21] these skeleton-keys include the all-purpose noun 'thing' [line 1] for 'item, plan, problem, event, etc.,' the all-purpose preposition 'on' [25] for 'in, for, by, of, concerning, etc.,' and finally the counting-approximaters 'about' [5, 6, 7] and 'or so' [24], both meaning 'approximately' (a formal word). Other consultative code-label skeleton-keys exist, but our sample is enough to show how they work. In line 1, good casual style would have had 'something else' and stiff formal style perhaps 'a situation which has arisen.' A formal jokester may pretend to get a ludicrous picture out of 'I'd like to see you on a typewriter'; the trained social animal simply takes 'on' as a code-label for informal consultation.

Both colloquial styles—consultative and casual—routinely deal in a public sort of information, though differently: casual style takes it for granted and at most alludes to it, consultative style states it as fast as it is needed. Where there happens to be no public information for a while, a casual conversation (among men) lapses into silences and kidding, a consultative one is broken off or adjourned. These adjustments help to show what sort of rôle public information plays in the two colloquial styles: it is essential to them both.

Now in intimate style, this rôle is not merely weakened; rather, it is positively abolished. Intimate speech excludes public information. (Then how can it be language? — Let's see: it's *Miss* Fidditch, isn't it?)

Definition: An intimate utterance pointedly avoids giving the addressee information from outside of the speaker's skin. Example: 'Ready' said in quite a variety of situations, some of them allowing other persons to be present; note that this could be equivalent to either a statement or a question; the manner of saying it will be described in a moment. Another: 'Engh' or 'Cold' said at the family supper-table, but not to tell the speaker's wife that the coffee is cold—as it would tell her after we let Miss Fidditch expand the ellipsis for us: wrongly, for this is not an ellipsis. This tells the speaker's wife nothing about the coffee. How could it! She knows exactly how long since it was hot. If she had had to be told, the casual-style 'Coffee's cold' would have been used instead. After all, they both know the code. The point of any such utterance is simply to remind (hardly 'inform') the addressee of some feeling (unspecified, but that does not matter) inside the speaker's skin. (But I do wish they would speak like human beings! — What else?)

The systematic features of intimate style are two, just as in the other styles: (1) extraction; (2) jargon. Both are stable, once the intimate group (normally a pair) has been formed. Extraction has just been illustrated: the speaker extracts a minimum pattern from some conceivable casual sentence. Extraction is not ellipsis. An elliptical sentence still has wording, grammar, and intonation. Intimate extraction employs only part of this triplet. Our printed 'Engh' represents an empty word, one that has no dictionary meaning but serves as a code-label for intimate style. (The parallel word in casual style, spelled 'unh,' has a different vocal quality.) There is, however, a message-meaning; this is conveyed by the intonation, the melody, with which 'Engh' is spoken. The speaker has extracted this intonation from a possible casual sentence, and that is all he uses of the grammatical triplet 'wording, grammar, intonation.' Again, our other example 'Cold' represents the word-identity alone, here spoken in a meaningless monotone; and the same is true of 'Ready.' In these instances, the triplet has been reduced to its first member, as 'Engh' reduced it to its last one, leaving the addressee to fill out the message—or, preferably, to comprehend it as it stands. (I couldn't. — Would you be so kind?)

Once more, this is not rudeness; this pays the addressee the highest compliment possible among mature people. Maturity implies some guardedness in public relations; here there is none, and the speaker is saying so. There is an exact discrimination between the inside and the outside of the speaker's skin; he makes this obvious, and pays the addressee the compliment of implying that she knows him inside and out. (Engh — It *is* . . . Miss Fidditch, isn't it?)

Intimate style tolerates nothing of the system of any other style: no slang, no background information, and so on. Any item of an intimate code that the folklore calls 'slang' is not slang but jargon—it is not ephemeral, but part of the permanent code of this group—it has to be, for intimacy does not tolerate the slang imputation that the addressee needs to be told that she is an insider. The imputations of all other styles are similarly corrosive. Accordingly, intimate codes, or jargons, are severely limited in their use of public vocabulary. Each intimate group must invent its own code. Somehow connected with all this is the cozy fact that language itself can never be a topic in intimate style. Any reaction to grammar, for instance, promptly disrupts intimacy. [S'mother time, M . . . F . . .]

IV

AN INFORMATIVE CLOCK

W<small>E</small> return briefly to consultative style. It supplies background information currently, and the listener participates fully. His participation insures that there shall be neither too little nor too much background given. If too little, he will break in to ask for elucidation; if too much, he may say 'yes I know.' The diction is kept in accurate balance with the requirements: the pronunciation is clear but does not clatter, the grammar is complete but for an occasional anacoluthon, the semantics is adequate without fussiness. All is adjusted by instantaneous homeostasis, and the speaker does not compose text more than two or three seconds in advance. He could not in any case, since he must expect the hearer to insert a word or two every six seconds. Being thus entirely automatic, it is the most strictly organized type of language. Its grammar is central to all the possibilities of grammar, and the grammars of all other styles are formed by adding archaisms and other complications to the consultative grammar; the pronunciations of all other styles are most simply described as departures from consultative pronunciation; the meanings of any word which occurs at all in consultative style are basically its consultative meanings, to which each other style adds specific meanings as necessitated by its own function: private meanings in intimate style, slang meanings in casual style, technical meanings in formal style, allusive meanings in frozen style.

Describing formal style by departure from consultative style, the crucial difference is that participation drops out. This is forced whenever the group has grown too large: the insertions then may overlap, causing semantic confusion, or each listener must space his insertions out beyond the biological limit of about thirty seconds; either of these results then causes this or that group-member to withdraw by becoming catatonic or absent, or to begin speaking in formal style and thus to render the others catatonic or absent. This homeostasis, then, either reduces the size of the group so that it may remain consultative or splits the group into one manic speaker and a set of catatonic hearers. A competent manic is able to convert a tête-à-tête into a formal assembly; but normal persons maintain consultation up to a group-size of approximately six, which sets the limits on the size and composition of a 'committee' in the English-speaking sense. Beyond that, parliamentary law is requisite, i.e. a division into active and chair-warming persons.

Non-participation is also forced whenever a speaker is entirely uncertain of the prospective response. Thus conversations between strangers begin in formal style; among urbane strangers in English-speaking cultures, the formal span is only the ceremony of introduction, whose function is to insure that no real business shall be impeded by formality; it then lasts for one consultative speech-span, approximately six seconds. Within a consultation, a similar formal span is instituted whenever embarrassment arises or is imminent. The rupture of consultation is marked either by formal leave-taking or by casual leave-taking; adjournment of consultation is marked by consultative leave-taking, e.g. 'I might not be back for a while.'

Formal style is designed to inform: its dominating character, something which is necessarily ancillary in consultation, incidental in casual discourse, absent in intimacy. The formal code-labels inform each hearer that he is in a formal frame, is not to make insertions but must wait until authorized to speak, and is being given time to plan reactions—as much as half a century. The leading code-label is 'may;' any message requiring either 'might' or 'can' in other styles is suppressed or paraphrased, giving 'May I help you?' and 'We may not see one another for some time,' the consultative equivalent of which was cited previously. We may most economically label an introduction as formal by saying 'May I present Mr. Smith?'—or petrify a child by saying 'No, you may not.' Originally, the well-placed 'may' was as effective as a hat-pin.

Beyond its code-labels, formal style is strictly determined by the absence of participation. This absence infects the speaker also. He may speak as if he were not present, avoiding such allusions to his own existence as 'I, me, mine,' with the possible exception of 'one'—a formal code-label—or 'myself' in desperate situations. The speaker protects both the text and himself from involvement; presumably he will be absent if the roof collapses.

Lacking all personal support, the text must fight its own battles. Form becomes its dominant character. Robbed of personal links to reality, it scorns such other links as the stone painfully kicked to refute an idealist philosopher; instead, it endeavors to employ only logical links, kept entirely within the text, and displays those logical links with sedulous care. The pronunciation is explicit to the point of clattering; the grammar tolerates no ellipsis and cultivates elaborateness; the semantics is fussy. Background information is woven into the text in complex sentences. Exempt from interruption, the text organizes itself into paragraphs; the paragraphs are linked explicitly: thus this is the third of a quadruplet.

Formal text therefore demands advance ← planning. Consultative speakers never plan more than the current phrase, and are allowed only a limited number of attempts to return to their muttons before abandoning them; the formal speaker has a captive audience, and is under obligation to provide a plan for the whole sentence before he begins uttering it, an outline of the paragraph before introducing it, and a delimitation of field for his whole discourse before he embarks on it. One who does all this currently, keeping the three levels of his planning under continuous control, is correctly said to think on his feet; for clearly it calls for something other than brains, and intelligent persons do not attempt it but instead have the text all composed and written out at leisure.

The defining features of formal style are two: (1) detachment; (2) cohesion. One feature, of the highest importance, is retained from the basal styles: intonation. Since the audience hears the text just once, any deficiency in the intonation is dangerous, any major defect is disastrous. Lack of intonation, as in print, is simply a blank check; but false intonation will mulct the listener in triple damages. In the formal frame a native speaker may say 'pine *tree*' with the second word loudest, insisting on an impossible message. The fog of confusion which this spreads over the listeners' attention will render approximately six subsequent words inaudible to them. Meanwhile they must first detect the absurdity of what they plainly heard; second, forget the pseudo-sentence but retain the list of its words in sequence; third, by trial and error construct a plausible sentence from that list. Such listening is known as 'a duty to onself,' and the monetary cost is deductible in income-tax returns.

V

A FORMATIVE CLOCK

THAT list of words in sequence is all that is left in frozen style. Punctuation is of very little help towards an adequate intonation, and good frozen style never relies on it. Frozen style—a style for print and for declamation—is defined by the absence of authoritative intonation in the text, as also by the fact that the reader or hearer is not permitted to cross-question the author. Relative to the other styles, these peculiarities clearly are defects in the frozen style, preventing it from functioning as they do. Freed from those other functions, frozen style develops its own functions, by common consent surpassing the others. From the surpassing excellence of good frozen style, our folklore has derived the mistaken theory that it is the ideal of all language.

Is not good writing the highest type of language? Yes, in its own way. But if we approach it through the Grove of Academe, we see nothing but trees labeled 'best' and 'correct' and 'classic' and the rest. It is not possible to discern the nature of excellence in memorable writing from the standpoint that fine printable style is a complex of correct forms and superior formulas. If that were true, it could be learned; the truth is that it can only be invented.

Frozen style can indeed be understood on its own terms, but only if the way is cleared of the prejudice that it does what other discourse does but does it better. To do that, we swiftly approach it twice from the other end of the style scale. Good intimate style fuses two personalities. Good casual style integrates disparate personalities into a social group which is greater than the sum of its parts, for now the personalities complement each other instead of clashing. Good consultative style produces cooperation without the integration, profiting from the lack of it. Good formal style informs the individual separately, so that his future planning may be the more discriminate. Good frozen style, finally, lures him into educating himself, so that he may the more confidently act what rôle he chooses.

Each of the latter four does its own work by making a virtue out of necessity—a necessity that springs from its own deficiencies in comparison to one or two basal styles. Personal disparities are over-compensated in social integration by casual devices designed out of the mere fact that one person is not another person. Each lack of shared information is over-compensated in consultation, because two heads are better than one and consultation makes them more than twice as good. Each loss from lack of participation is over-compensated in good formal communication by giving several hours of preparation to one hour of discourse.

Frozen style is for people who are to remain social strangers. Our direct compensation for remaining strangers is consultative style. By comparison, frozen style lacks two things, participation and intonation. It gains two things of which this is one: the reader can reread.

Let this word not be misunderstood. Rereading is not re-scanning the print. Re-scanning is the least profitable substitute for rereading, and is best reserved for official documents. Rereading is reconsidering the text. It is best done with the eyes closed. It can be done thousands of miles and thousands of days distant from the printed page.

The reader can reread. In the one fact lies both the writer's opportunity and his danger. If he has not somehow trained himself to his proper task, he will simply lay a fixed message out neatly into sentences, so that they can be fully understood with one re-scanning, so clear and shallow are they. That is only excellent formal style. It will not do the work of even a poor frozen style.

The opportunity is that the writer who is dedicated can enable the rereader to educate himself indefinitely far beyond what the writer put into the text in the first place. The writer only initiates the process; then the rereader carries on from there. What is the writer's part? To rewrite. The writer is a rewriter, or he is no proper writer at all—like Thomas Wolfe. Non-writers have their function too, but that is not what we are concerned with now.

The rewriter is not the man who revises for clarity and force in a message once chosen complete, seeking to clothe it decently. When that is undertaken and well executed, we learn with sorrow that he has not only laid the garment of his thought out handsomely but has laid out the body too. ('Not only' before 'has,' or delete the second 'has.' — Sorry, Miss Fidditch; I will not kill an innocent thought unless you give me a better one. — But that would be clear and correct! — But he's just as dead as if he'd been wrong.)

The rewriter is as one who packs his thought for a long journey. Having packed the garment, he does not merely straighten out the folds and close the paragraph. Instead, he unpacks completely and repacks again. And again; and again and again. Each time, he tucks just one more thought into this or that pocket. When he quits, there are more of them than of words. So many labors of love on a single sentence, that many rewards for the rereader. On the surface, one teasing half-reward; others at successively greater and greater depths, so that each reading finds one more. (Why whatever for? — Reread and see.)

Conceivably those successive depths might be achieved in one writing; but more probably the genius is simply the man who can do the repacking inside his skull. In any case, there must be repacking with more ideas insinuated into the wording. The rewards will lie at successive depths only if they were packed into the text in successive repackings. That is simply the kind of wits we have.

The rereader's wits do not directly reverse the process. The last-packed idea may be the second discovered then, and so on in a sequence that is likely to agree partly with the sequence of packings and partly with the reverse sequence. There is no good reason for preferring either direction. When the rereader reverses the rewriter's sequence, he profits from the harmony between their wits; when he follows it direct, he profits from their disparities; and if he skips a step, he strengthens his wits by the exercise.

Because the present report does not suffer from enough modesty to delay the proceedings, a rewriter's share of the transaction may be illustrated from a parenthesis near the top of page 9. The drafts that can be resurrected ran thus:

Excuse us, please.

Quiet, Miss Fidditch.

Quiet, Miss F; the children are studying.

Quiet, there! These are people, studying for exams.

Quiet there, Miss Fidditch. These people are studying.

Quiet there, Miss F. These are people preparing for examinations.

The increasing length bears witness to this writer's amateur standing. Still, there is enough here to make the point. The text is short enough to be read at once as a whole. Then the number of rescannings can easily be far less than the number of readings: each discovery of another meaning counts as one more rereading if there was any delay whatever. Probably this line was reconsidered a good half-dozen times by each rereader among the readers of the page where it is at home. (There! I knew it was obscure! — No comment for the present.)

Next, we must recognize that the rereader has a right to congratulate himself for each new meaning that he finds. There is no essential difference between discovery and invention, and every new thought is compounded and distilled from old memories. To make a centaur, you do need a man and a horse, and yet you are a brave boy when you've done it. The rereader is a creative thinker. He is thoroughly justified in feeling that he has created a half-dozen meanings in reconsidering a text too short to hold them all on its surface. He will feel that; it would be inhuman not to. (Don't you mean 'unhuman' or 'nonhuman?' — 'Inhumane' if you say so!)

But—he was lured on into doing it. Definition: Good frozen style is whatever lures the reader on and on through successive inventive discoveries. It is good in the sense that it is a germ and a contagion of good. It starts a process whose continuing is a good thing; it gives momentum to insure the continuing. The reader, rewarded for several successive acts of creative thinking with one reward for each, gets into the swing of it and continues creating more and more meanings to suit his convenience; then he is educating himself.

This is not obscurity in the text, for obscurity breaks off the sequence too early or blocks it from ever starting. This is not clarity, for clarity allows no such sequence to start itself; the reader's own effort must develop the momentum, and the writer's effort can not do it for him. All the writer can do is to repack somewhere between obscurity and clarity.

Fortunately for the dedicated writer, there is a full wide space between the two, within which honest work can achieve respectable small effects like this one every time he tries and where he more or less frequently may make a lucky hit. He need not worry about exactly suiting an imagined reader; after all, what is too much repacking for one prospective reader will be too little for another, and each rewriter gets the audience he deserves. Whether he consciously knows it or not, each writer selects his stable audience by what sorts of things he insinuates and how many of them—not by his surface message. For example, the ninth word of this paragraph will say nothing to one reader, will mean one thing to the next but suggest nothing further, will for a third reader simply add an archaic flavor, will offer an illuminating analogy to a fourth reader, and will start an indefinitely long chain of associations within the fifth. Assuming that the writer is reconciled to having his subconscious select his audience for him—that is to say, assuming that he is mature—the only way he could lose in this transaction is that the fifth man's associations might lead him into a snake-pit of painful memories. But that must happen sooner or later if it can happen at all, and in principle it is independent of the initiating text. The all-human catalog of painful memories is infinite in size and variety, so that no writer can usefully plan to avoid them at all. (I try to tell my pupils not to offend people unnecessarily. — I suppose so.)

Adequately started, the rereader's momentum carries him on—perhaps even for decades —on and on indefinitely far beyond what the writer could decently claim credit for having put into the printed text. Wise writers may discover this fact consciously too, but then they usually keep it a secret: they either have always known or promptly discover that the lay public can't endure to face the truth of the matter and will protect themselves against it by classifying the author's plain statement as a joke or an attempt at obfuscation. Thus Browning on a poem of his earlier years: 'When I wrote that, only God and Robert Browning knew what it meant, and now only God knows.' And Goethe, when asked which of two interpretations of an early poem of his was correct: 'After all, why not?' Some critics know the fact too; but most of them are reluctant to expose it for fear of seeming to be trying to start a new criticism school. (My pupils keep asking me what poems mean. — The guessing is fun, isn't it?)

Therefore, if attention is called, a little later on here, to some possible rereadings of our sample of rewriting, it is not by way of boasting. A writer can at most claim credit for a first push onto an unpredictable path of self-education through rereading and beyond. He deserves neither credit nor blame for what length or turnings that path may develop later. Accordingly, good writers don't have to be perfect; and no man, not even the present reporter, need feel any shame for going to print with an honest day's work. If he has allowed for enough

successive rewards to lure some few readers beyond a first reading, he can draw his pay with
a clear conscience. (I have some favorite au-
thors that most people don't think much of. —
Are they alive? Rewrite and tell them!)

In an obvious sense, consummate formal
writing is a waste of time for the reader. When
all the writer's own ideas are forced upon the
reader, who could protect himself against them
only by inattention, no rereading momentum
can develop. Apparently everything by Winston
Churchill is like that. (My aunt thinks his writing is just wonderful. — So did he.)

No. Good writing is not the perfectly tailored
garment of a Personage, perfectly pressed since
last he wore it; it is the rumpled suit of a living
person, still relaxing from the strain of his
labors, its pockets stuffed with trash and with
things worth getting at. And each thing gets its
value from the finder. (I'll have to think that
over. — Good.)

Besides rereading, there is something of its
own kind to be called refeeling. When this
occurs alone, the text is promptly thrust behind,
recoiling from the push it gave, while the re-
feeler pursues his own nostalgias alone. The
style may be speciously like frozen style, but
it is not the same thing, as formal style is and

is not; indeed, this may be called 'anti-formal style because it reverses the aims of formal style by subordinating information to involvement. Confusingly, anti-formal style is found in two opposite varieties, namely as emitted by non-writers, like Thomas Wolfe, who simply fill the text with salt tears, and by over-writers, like Franz Kafka and Edgar Allan Poe, who stew and distill so as to fill it with nothing but ardent spirits. In such case, the reader finds that the ship has sunk with all hands that he himself is rolling and tumbling, floating alone on a crumbling cask with nothing to drink but rum and sea-water, fit only to inflame his thirst. In one thirsty gulp the unwary reader will utterly drain the text to fill his feelings. Then the cask collapses, the sea is a desert; there is no text left to be reread. One is alone: to re-scan the print, yes, if lust prevails over wisdom; but that will only start up the old lonesome feelings over and over, to go their own road again, a way perchance fascinatingly uncharted—but now it never will be charted, without any text. That is not the way to profit from the second advantage of frozen style: that it can be refelt as well as reread. (But *The Raven* was lovely! — Do you regress often?)

Yet there is a wise way, an adequate balance of rereading and refeeling. This comes about when the text and feelings are first not too far from equally worth reconsidering; then the reader promptly brings them into balance; then their double pursuit never abandons either the one or the other. This double process is initiated in the adequate reader by genuine poetry and by dedicated prose.

Only by virtue of this balance is it possible for the pursuit of feelings to transcend both crude facts and raw lust and go on into another country: wisdom. The reason is that we are not only thinkers but feeling thinkers, not only animals but speaking animals. Our kind of wisdom implicates and is implicated by text, and likewise implicates and is implicated by feelings. Feelings and text are inseparable in human wisdom. Not just the text first seen in print or heard, and the feelings first rousing themselves then, but also—and rather—the continuations created by one who refeels and rereads them together in their indissoluble marriage. And this wisdom is the esthetic of literature.

Definition: Literature is that text which the community insists on having repeated from time to time intact. It is created in its success. When the community refuses to reread and re-feel a composition, it is not a literary text; it remains a draft. (We must wait and see! — See if we want to reread it.)

What intactness must be is clear. It is whatever constancy in the text preserves its marriage with the community feeling for it. Diverging versions—of text, of community feeling, of personal self-placement—divide and unite genres and also sub-communities. In a stable and evolving culture, the balance between division and union keeps all the entities healthy. (Homeostasis? — After all, why not?)

In unwritten literatures, as the culture evolves through the generations and the catastrophes, feelings evolve under that law continuously. When the feelings drift right along with the culture, the text keeps in step by modernizing itself continuously; example: any medieval ballad of Scottish border tragedy and its modern versions referring to feuds in our eastern mountains. (I don't know why, but I like them. — You don't need to, and I'm glad.)

When the values drift down certain slopes to occupy swampy areas continuously depopulated by the disintegration of texts, the text becomes vulgar and less stable; example: any

Boccaccio's tale and the immensely numerous and variable anecdotes of today stemming therefrom. (I try not to listen. — So you do hear them? Good: there's vitamins in them—they grow in rich muck.)

When the values similarly drift upward on certain slopes to occupy uplands repeatedly depopulated by the disintegration of feelings, the text becomes constitutional and more stable; example: any sacred book. Then that sub-community which feels able to follow the rising feelings becomes smaller and develops a more intense pride in the possession of the mystery—which swiftly completes the alienation from the community feeling norm: the text is now hieratic and forever fixed. (How long is that? — While the community is intact.)

When, finally—and this fourth case joins with the first—the feelings diverge sidewise instead of down or up, the text becomes obsolete and vanishes, as a whole, through lack of demand for its intact repetition; example: any ancient hero-tale which didn't happen to be written down in time. (*The Mabinogion!* — What there's left of it.)

Then the disintegrating text is treated as a grab-bag of fragments, of all sizes down to single words and even shapes of words, to be patched into and onto any tale apt to be adorned by them. When patched onto, they give at least two layers of depth at once, to start the rereading and refeeling process and to teach writers what depth may be; and by appealing to nostalgias they provide the requisite first surface values. (I'm just in love with old English ballads. — Right you are.)

Now the community is free to reread and refeel the well-patched text into an above-average status with respect to sufficient sub-community norms of feeling; then it is classical; examples: Icelandic family sagas and the Paul Bunyan cycle. (I read a Paul Bunyan collection recently, but I think there are some fakes in it. — You can tell, can't you!)

Description amounting to a definition: Classical text is that text which has been spun from a thread of feeling, woven close to a community pattern of feeling, tailored to suit rereadings of men and events, patched with pieces that would not have been taken while the brands were still visible, and worn long enough to prove that it will wear. (Why isn't that your five clocks? — Come to think of it, you're right! Thank you, Miss Fidditch, I mean Candida.)

When a next-succeeding text is made in this way, the thread and tissue of actual feelings must sew and piece it. This living material is apt to form the most cherished parts for the time being. Cherishing them makes them hardy, and they can survive to achieve their second life in the next fragmentation, when the former fragments have been discarded as text and are gone to the pulping-mill. (Linen paper? — Bleached rag body, fit for any writing: semantics, grammar, phonology.)

And so on forever and ever, with never more need to invent a totally new tale than to make a man in a laboratory. The whole process is automatic. Communities have always found it easier to maintain literature than factual history, and the most stable texts referring to actual men and events are always the mythical texts like the patched-up tale of George Washington and his cherry-tree. (I keep trying to get my students to be original. — Why how do you do, Miss Frankenstein!)

The definition again: Literature is that text which the community insists on having repeated from time to time intact, and the word 'intact' has just been reread. It is the key word here. It seems to answer to some instinct or other, for each child, once he is old enough to follow a tale at all, insists that repetitions must occur and must occur in the identical wording. It is as if the child was born knowing what mature people imagine they found out by developing a taste for classical literature: that self-education best starts out repeatedly from the identical text. But this coincidence ought not to surprise us. Anthropologists, by analysing many . . . (That manic is here again! — Sorry; thank you.)

With the parallel growth of printing and of monster nations, a text can survive on paper if only one person in a thousand buys a copy once in his lifetime. Then arithmetic says that there could be a thousand literary genres in a single nation. But the most popular genre, what with advertising and all that—in ancient times already the varying choices of hearers and the reputation of this or that literary cloth or tailor —is sure to claim some large fraction of the market; then the next one can claim a large fraction of the remainder, and on and on until the residue will not be large enough to pay for printing or for a minstrel's supper. Today, the result is something like ten genres: the comic books for one, *Readers Digest* for another, and so on. (I prefer . . . — Of course: we all do.)

Let us pick a genre at random, and get on with it. We go back to the point that the text is to be unfrozen by reconsidering it; a text that does not require unfreezing is not in frozen style and we need not consider it, any more than a reader will reconsider it. (I hope the random choice appeals to me. — We aim to please, Candida.)

If a man who reads *Hamlet* a hundred times is a more faithful devotee of literature than one who reads *Hamlet* ten times, then the narratives of baseball games claim one of the largest bodies of rereaders intensely devoted to literature; for they insist that the texts must read so nearly alike that one who has let slip a few random facts will glance at the date to make sure it isn't yesterday's paper. It is clear that one profits thrillingly from the thousandth departure from the same text. (You can't be serious! — How do you know I can't?)

Baseball is a highly literary game. Its rereader, knowing that the players need not be superlative athletes as in tennis or soccer, feels no bar to identifying with them—a necessity of literature. The rules are intricate to the point of inscrutability; the events are various enough to simulate the complexity of life itself. Then our normal reluctance to face complexities can equalize the comprehensions of life and of baseball, facilitating the just balance of text and feelings for continuing joint reconsideration: by definition, then, baseball text is dedicated prose. The lexicon is rich and strictly organized, yet with ample room for tropes—which are not slang because the business is known to be serious. The same event may be narrated with immense variety, the same patch of text will cover an infinite number of events—for who can doubt that baseball will endure as long as apple pie? (How long is that? — Same answer.)

Then since it doesn't matter whether we take a baseball text or any other sample of frozen style, we return to page 44. We have seen what the rewriting looks like as factual history; now how about a literary myth to clothe it? (Why not the truth, the whole . . . — What is truth?)

Here goes, then. Suppose the writer has chosen a message; how can he compensate for the absence of intonation if nothing more? In principle, there are two separate methods, though in practice they are routinely combined. One method is to choose and arrange words that will do their work without relying on intonation; and the other is to force an adequate intonation. And remember that these methods, combined or separately, must accomplish the rewriter's task: packing several ideas down and down, where they can be discovered later and later. (I'm holding my breath. — Keep your fingers crossed too, Candida.)

Take the word 'preparing.' First its value independent of intonation, a value or values which may emerge sooner or later as the re-reader experiments with the text and feelings. On those grounds, and assuming, as the writer must, that the rereader is his own twin, the word 'preparing' was chosen for two sorts of effects. For one thing, it would be more persuasive to our hypothetical Miss F than 'studying' or perhaps any other word that might have suited the dramatic occasion; this may lure the reader into reconsidering his image of Miss F and what makes her tick, a reconsidering which may be renewed as he comes to think of her and of her sisters either on real-life occasions or on literary ones, again and again into the indefinite future. For another thing, it was intended to lure the reader into side-slips, such as thinking of 'preparation for living' as the P.T.A. calls it, then into reconsidering the future lives of young members of one's own family, specifically perhaps from the amusing departure of thinking what an 'examination' might be in that context—a proposal of marriage—trying for a job where 'Toots' would

disqualify—selecting a girl who 'doesn't criticize' (forming a group that will be homogeneous on the responsibility scale)—choosing an
ambitious husband—and so on and on; and
then departing again, from any link, down other
association-chains. If some reader of that text
or of this paragraph calls this the main message
and calls the other one the side-slips, the writer
will be the last man to object. (Do you mean
to say that writers don't know what they're
saying? — Yes;)

Second, the contribution of 'preparing'
toward forcing an adequate intonation. The
word 'people' had been chosen previously; now
the problem was to prevent its being taken as
a synonym for 'children.' The obvious solution
is to not only make it loud, which English
grammar otherwise does already, but leave it
marked with a pregnant pause—a pause which
says that the preceding word is to be taken in
its most intense meanings. Such a pause is an
English comma-pause; now the problem is to
force one. (Note the word 'English' here; this
sort of transaction is a large part of what we
mean when we say 'literature is untranslat-
able.') Now listen to the sequence 'people preparing.' It contains four successive syllables
beginning with [p]. (Shade of Macaulay! — I

hope he's as happy wherever he's at home.) Again, in the middle there is the dark English [1] sound. Now a series of four [p] syllables in this English rhythm will force a pause midway; and then the dark [1] will force the dipping intonation which makes this an English comma-pause. This comma-pause, finally, makes 'people' pregnant, as required by the conditions of our whole problem. (You can't mean you knew you were doing all that! — How should I know what I can mean?)

A comma there is [,] now no longer needed. There is no great harm in printing the comma in prose; but a poet would be justified in striking it out in galley-proof, with the same reason as for not using italics. Simply printing the comma without having forced the pause by the wording is a surrender in ignominious defeat. If only shallow wordings, or wordings which will not force a useful intonation, can be found for the first message thought of, the writer must start all over again, hoping to hit upon another message of greater promise. (What's the matter? Don't you . . . — You mean to say that writers don't care what they say just so they say at least two things at once? Why, that's . . . Oh, never mind; I think I'll just take an aspirin and . . .)

The writer invites defeat whenever he takes on the double burden of placing a certain message complete within a certain span of text. Postponement is wiser, at least for the most important messages; for then they will invade the text all along meanwhile, pervading its suppressions and ambiguities with a tincture of expectancy. It would be hard to accomplish that by plan; it is easy to let it happen: just postpone, and it happens anyhow. (Good writing can't be planned? — Believe *The Raven* if you like, but not Poe's essay on it!)

Trivialities can be planned, for instance the question that elicited the answer 'Yes;' not long ago, signifying: (1) They know what they are saying. (2) I mean they don't know. (3) You have asked a dear sweet four-year-old's unanswerable question; I will answer accordingly and hope you'll be content and go away to play. (I like that! — Thank you.)

A more complex example is the answer to a more recent question, designed to be entirely at the mercy of the reader's intonation so that it can be taken absolutely any way he likes. At least eight ways of taking it are given by choice of accented syllable; in the printed versions here, the chosen word is italicized without meaning over-emphasis—simply to locate the choice for the reader:

> How should I know what I can *mean* when I don't even know . . .
>
> How should I know what I *can* mean unless I try?
>
> How should I know what *I* can mean when I don't know what . . .
>
> How should I know *what* I can mean—quite a lot so far!
>
> How should I *know* what I can mean when I feel I must guess?
>
> How shouid *I* know what I can mean—ask the experts!
>
> How *should* I know what I can mean if not this way?
>
> *How* should I know what I can mean? You shall teach me.

Now multiply by two, because it was either 'mean in the text under consideration' or else 'mean during the present reconsideration'; that makes 16. Then pick a number and multiply by that, since not all fluent continuations have been printed here, and again because some continuations may also be ambiguous. (Pretty vague! — Would you recognize vagueness in a . . . no; sorry; that was rude of me.)

No, this is not vagueness. To be vague is to be rude; and this is not rudeness. It is, indeed, exactly what was called 'not rudeness' in considering the two familiar styles. This ambiguity is the special politeness of frozen style. The rewriter does not force the reader to swallow a single message. (Ambiguity again! Aw, I give up! — Come on; relax and enjoy it.)

This Bluebeard has told the reader exactly the same thing as her mother must have told her—to open any door but one in the sprawling castle he has provided for her. If instead he had turned her out to forage for herself during his absence, that would have been vagueness, that would have been rudeness. (Bluebeard—and Mr. Rochester! — Fine! Reread more!)

The rewriter treats the rereader as one who is equally human; he deserves to be paid in the same coin. He feels, as the reader must, that we can understand only what we can say. The only messages a literary writer can possibly put over, in any case, are those inventively discovered by the reader. In his most broadly ambiguous text, he is at his most thorough; he is most mindful of his duty when he gives each rereader perfect freedom to create the most profitable messages. (But it makes me feel so insecure! — How do you think I feel?)

His other duty—in the sense that it is a politician's first duty to get himself elected—is to provide the first allurements. He need not always provide equally many of them: certain readers profit most when they must even break into the castle before they will wander in it. From that to the opposite extreme—those who want only surface gold, and wouldn't do a day's digging themselves for a million—the readers are spread out in a broad spectrum. The writer can choose his reader-companions along the whole length of this responsibility-scale, as we always form our social groups. (I try so hard, and . . . — Knock at some other door, Candida.)

But there is no use having a scale unless you know which way is up. It is your reporter's choice to say that the top is where the text and the feelings can be made, in an adequate reader, equally worth reconsidering, and the total depth is as much as a lifetime of reconsidering needs. The Gettysburg Address is deep enough; and Robert Frost will do. And he'll do and he'll do. How much more, this respondent has not yet lived long enough to know. (Then . . .? — I hope you're as young as you look right now, Candy.)

Now there was that question of good literary form. Let's take it as an honest question and suppose that 'fine writing' was not meant. The answer is that there is no such thing as good literary form; there is only literary good form. It is all a question of politeness. (Oh . . . Thank you!)

Good form is that behavior which makes your partner feel at home; that's why literature is about people and the best literature is all about people. The ceremony of introduction must signal to the reader what kind of house and what kind of company he is getting into. And thereafter he is not to be treated like one who has wandered into the wrong house and company by mistake. Unless you choose for your house-guests only such persons as can feel at home in a practical joker's house. (— You're welcome.)

Tell him 'black tie' or 'sport clothes' when you are inviting him; introduce him to a company who are reasonably well assorted among themselves, and don't replace them with a different set overnight so that he sees only unplaceable strangers at breakfast. Since you are a member of the community, you'll know what to do. (Oh, I do hope so . . . — Come on, we're all with you.)

Definition: Literary good form is whatever keeps the reader feeling at home. More later. (Oh, wait a minute! May I understand that correct spelling is good form? — You might. You may if you can. I'm inclined to feel so myself. —

VI

THE BEST BUTTER

. . . I have not slept at all well recently, perhaps because I am worried. Ever since Mother died I have had only two things for which to live, and now it appears that both are in serious danger. I want Babe (she does not like me to call her that, particularly in private—why should it be that way around?—and really she is anything but a baby now) to marry her Stephen. I think he is a very promising young man. I have never heard him tell any of those stories where one of us could hear him at least. Last week, however, I caught him teasing Babe unmercifully. Evidently he was endeavoring to enrage her so that she would forget her upbringing and tell him off properly. She does not seem to understand that he may be trying to escape and does not wish to take the blame for breaking off with her. It makes me ill to think of it. Where shall I find another. The other problem is that I have caught three of my rowdiest English (I can see that that sounds strange, but I am too distraught for correcting) students making parodies on the Portia speech, the one I have always loved. Really! If I cannot instil a proper respect for Shakespeare in my own students, I feel that I am simply wasting my time as a teacher of English and literature. Still, at my age, what else is there for me to do? Can you persuade Martin to write to me? His letters often seem rather rude at first sight, but when I reread them they are strangely comforting, though I do not know why. . . . I am thinking of returning to work upon my dissertation. Perhaps I shall buy a new hat. I tried washing my hair last night, but that did not seem to do as much good as usually.

For crying out loud! What's the matter with you? Didn't your mother teach you anything? I know that when they get married you will be ecstatic about it, probably because Stephen is almost nephew spelled backwards, but never mind about that, since any reason is a good reason to begin with and I agree about Stephen and Babe because he is a normal specimen.

Yet you are worried—because he teases her! What really ought to worry you is if he bought her a corsage chosen by price without looking twice at it, hired a car to take her to the Club dance, treated her with formal politeness—and turned her over to some wolf to dance with while he went over to that wallflower, started a conversation on his favorite topic (chemistry, isn't it?) and then as adroitly as if subconsciously (probably would be) worked the conversation around to where he got her angry enough at him to take off her glasses. That would indeed portend disaster for the family. Not that there aren't other young men, but because it could mean that maybe nobody will want to tease your sister. And you are worried because you have caught some of your students trying to outdo each other, in working out parodies on Portia's speech. You ought to be dancing in the streets. As long as they treat Shakespeare with that formal respect which my own high-school teacher required, you must know that they will escape from his company at the earliest opportunity. But if they play with Portia until they turn 'strained' into 're-strained, Honey!' I believe you are smart enough to realize that he has gotten under their skin, and sooner or later—never mind, half a lifetime is still soon enough on the average—they will at least subconsciously feel what Portia meant; and if one of them turns into a philologist he will corner you one day after you have retired and earnestly explain to you that 'strained' for 'restrained, constrained' is the same deal as 'cute,' for 'acute,' with suitable Greek terminology. You are afraid that there is no limit to what this parodying may lead to. Well, you can thank your stars there is not. It can even—if it can't, nothing can—turn one or two of your chemists into poets, on the side or straight (I like mixtures myself), mayhap give us another Shakespeare in due course. There is no limit. When you visit us at Christmas—can you bring Babe along or won't she leave Stephen?—and we are singing past the Christmas hymns through our favorites for their harmonies, I will point out a hymn which I could quote exactly here but which I will not because, taken straight, it still reminds me too much of castor oil. What I will quote is the parody I picked up from a young hell-raiser ('scamp' your mother would have called him) who is now a clergyman: 'At the bar, at the bar, where I smoked my first cigar, and the burden of my heart rolled away! It was there by chance that I tore my Sunday pants, and now I wear them every day.' I am convinced that the reason he still wears them every day is that they were properly torn in his youth. I don't think he has had them invisibly mended; he is a good clergyman, and our janitor is a drunk (former) that he saved for us. And it has saved the hymn for me too—pickled it, you might say—for it is better poetry than the official version. Come to think of it, we might . . .

. . . The fluoridation referendum went against us after all the . . . My headaches have started again, and thinking about them only makes them worse. Mother was a martyr to them, and sometimes I think . . . I have taken a reading on the situation, as Stephen would call it (where do they get those things?) and I think I shall not try our little experiment. Stephen, strangely, is distressed, whether by the situation or by my timidity I am sure I could not say. The boys do not seem to care. I think they are working on limericks. Dare I hint that the Rubayyat form holds some promise? . . . That Superintendent has been here again, and this time he has a new complaint against us. That is to say, we thought it was new, but afterward we learned that he has been complaining of the same problem in all the schools this year. After visiting classes throughout the High School, he went to the Principal and asked why the twelfth grade students speak exactly as the ninth grade. He wishes to be informed whether we teach them no English at all during three years. They make such good progress in the grade schools. When, however, they enter High School, they begin to speak slang, and all progress ceases. As soon as the children enter Junior High, they seem to have forgotten everything good which they were taught previously. They pick up slang from both Divisions of the High School, and otherwise they lapse into incoherent mumbling and gabbling. I mean the boys do one and the girls do the other. There must be something in it, for I have often been charmed by the fluency and clarity of most eight year old children. Naturally, they do not yet speak as I should wish them to speak, but they are rarely at a loss and we can always tell exactly what they are trying to say. I have often envied the Third Grade teachers. At all events, the Principal has requested me to prepare a report, and what shall I say? He is sweet, and I am not worried about him; but what can we tell the Superintendent? . . . I overheard a rather good limerick the other day. I must re-

member to tell it to your wife at Christmas.
At present I cannot seem to edit it enough to
write it down without taking out whatever it is
that makes it good? At my age . . . I have had
no headache today, and I thought I should
certainly have one because of the Superintendent.

You can't tell him anything. Before he got
that job, he had to get a document first, with
a gilt seal, certifying that he was all through
being told. But if you get the story straight for
yourself, you've got a good chance of meeting
each new contretemps of that kind on its own
terms. Don't worry about it—your intuition will
tell you what to do when the time comes—
after all, you have survived so far. But I wish
you'd write and tell me afterwards what it was
that you did. The operations of the female
mind always fascinate me, and I find myself
welcoming contributions from anywhere at all
(though you are my favorite source now, Candida, outside of my family), even though I
ought to be getting plenty of them at home.

I'm not sure where I ought to begin the story,
but that has never mattered in the past, so I'll
begin it with the fourth of my six sisters. At
fifteen months, when she was already more

competent in English than our family average (and we all began to speak before we could walk without holding on) she decided, it seems, that this language was worth learning properly. We never used baby-talk to a younger person after they learned to smile, but rather spoke adult English clearly and at a moderate tempo, using sentences of not over two clauses and approximately a seven-year-old vocabulary. In short, we dealt respectfully with the language and with the person too. She is a food-chemist now and a good mother. You didn't know her as a small baby, but first when she was about five and would come to an older person with two or more other children together, listen expressionlessly to the answer to the spokesman's question, depart alone as they ran off together to play, and finally return twenty minutes later, alone, with the right question. Then she would join the others again. At fifteen months, I believe, she was exactly like that. So what did she do? Never mind; I'll tell you: trust me for that. I don't know the figures, but I believe about one baby in a hundred does it, though few of them for so long a period as she did. She clammed up. For a year and a half, to age thirty-three months, she spoke not one word. Her utterances then were only the standard murmurs, which she used with exquisite skill. Papa and mama were momentarily worried when we determined that she didn't speak in solitude either, but promptly relaxed after a home-made test of her comprehension. As I recall it, we noticed once that she had probably not been wearing her crossed-eye glasses for some two hours, and we were distractedly searching; but then I asked her for a conference, told her what I thought she had been doing for those two hours, and then strolled after her as she swiftly crept (too much in a hurry to try walking) through two rooms into a third, pulled herself up by a window-sill, and confidently reached behind an obscuring curtain, without looking, to the exact spot where she had laid her glasses two hours earlier. She had been about to do something which might have harmed them. We never did find out what that was, though she easily made her motive clear to us. She was then not yet eighteen months old.

I've got to hurry to catch my plane. More later.

I have just learned the limerick about the Nipponese poet, though I am told that it has been going the rounds for years:

A certain young man of Japan
wrote verses that never would scan;
    and when they asked why,
    he replied, 'Because I
arways try to get as many words into the rast
    rine as I possibry can.'

I tried it on my favorite rowdy, though I do not know why I should bother, for I am sure that he will be first a football player and then an insurance salesman. His reception of it was puzzling. He looked at me doubtfully, thanked me politely for something quite different which I had done for him much earlier, and went off by himself. . . . I have been free of headaches for two weeks now. I hope your journey was pleasant and profitable. . . . Stephen is still teasing Babe. He seems to be able to do it with a single word now. Strangely, she seems to prefer it that way too, and tries to play up.

Congratulations! Just don't try, please, to plan their honeymoon for them; it is evident that they will be thoroughly competent to do it themselves.

Your favorite rowdy was acting just like my baby sister, as I see it, as near as he could at his age. You suddenly became a useful puzzle to him; simultaneously, he saw that he might do well to reconsider his theory of literature; the combination was too much for him to take immediately, so he regressed a few hours and escaped. He may or may not be back with the right question later, but in any case he can be a better insurance salesman now. You have a right to be puzzled, and a duty too; for you shall tell me whether my tentative theory was wrong as soon as you know. But now my sister.

I was the first person she spoke to, after she decided that she had learned the language. It was seven in the evening and one of us, returning from the cellar, had left the door standing open wide. She had watched them go past as she stood right there; and now she turned to me where I sat five feet away and said, with exactly the right loudness for that distance, crystal-clear and with a five-year-old's tempo: 'Shall I shut the door?' Nobody else heard; I recovered (I hope) before she was too much affected by my amazement and said something like 'Yes, Lora, please shut the door.' Then I slyly informed the rest of us, and they knew what to do: they did a noble Stanislavski job of pretending that she had always spoken like that, and started asking her for advice and information.

I call what she did 'imprinting;' yes, I know that the word has another sense—some day, ask me about the geese and the meadowlarks (you can tell Babe or I can tell Stephen about that after they are married), the spectrograms and the United Press story and the patriots and the returned letters—but it's my language as well as Humpty-Dumpty's.

Tell me this—you are the right sex and a teacher too—when our Sherry was ten and her teachers had started to work on English, she suddenly got fascinatingly moral about my 'Ain't I?' but about nothing else; yet I was able to learn that there was quite a long list of shibboleths; why did she not set about curing me of them all? More than that: when I taxed her with neglect, she said, with every appearance of honesty, that 'ain't' was all they cared about in her school

HOW COULD YOUR BABY SISTER LEARN HOW TO
  ARTICULATE PLEASE

SHE ALWAYS WAS A FASTIDIOUS EATER AND DRANK
FROM BOTTLES

I have been working on your Sherry problem, and it becomes more and more complex
as I think about it. However, out of my teaching experience I believe that I can offer one
thought which at least has the merit of simplicity. Sherry must have really like her
teacher; the list of shibboleths was too long to
remember in its entirety; by using one outstand-
ing sample—and I know of nothing that would
horrify a ten year old child more than the pros-
pect of a lifetime with a father who says 'ain't'
and drinks out of bottles (so there!)—she was
doing her duty, both to her father and to the
'loco parentis' as Professor Batchellor used to
call us teachers. I had to study Child Psychol-
ogy in the Normal School; but it was difficult
to follow because it was diluted for us, I believe, and now I am rather insecure about it.
However, what I really meant to write was that
Sherry was able to use the most important thing
to substitute for them all; then she hid the
others all away in her subconscious mind where
she could always find them if she ever needed
them; and finally she assuaged her guilty feeling about hiding them, by promising herself

that she would be sure to use them when she was older? Is that clear? I wish I knew how to write as you do. When I try to diagram your sentences, there is often something left over with which I do not know what to do with; and yet they seem to make sense, and more sense when I think less about the grammar. I must stop thinking about that. I may get another headache. . . . I have also been doing some research on the limerick problem, because I feel sure that there is something hidden there which I, as a teacher, should discover. Strangely, my research consists entirely of looking at the boys and their doings—what I can see of them— with an interest which has risen to fascination and then to respect. I am sure that I have always respected children, but this feels differently. Today I went so far that (I must ask you to keep this a secret) I hid myself away in the University Library and read baseball stories, week after week and year after year, in the newspaper files. I thought that three hours of it would surely give me a headache, but instead I came out with a strange exalted feeling as if I had been to church.

I did not mail this letter yesterday because there seemed to be something more to say if I could only find the words. Now it is Sunday and I have been to church after all—I go about once a month, which I suppose is not often enough for a teacher—and I feel better about the limerick problem, though I do not see the connection. I did not get good grades in the course in Logic in the Summer School. . . . Last night I woke up at about three o'clock with a sentence which I felt I simply must write down. I hesitate to tell you what it is, because when I looked at it this morning I could not make head or tale of what I had written. Nevertheless, I still feel that there is some sort of truth hidden in it and that I should be able to find it in time. Perhaps I shall have another dream and shall be able to compare the two to find the greatest common divisor. Joseph had to do that, did he not? At all events, here is what I wrote: 'The young are all classicists.' Now make what you will of that. I wash my hands of it. Riddle me my dream, Joseph!

Candy, I just love you! And when I run out of wives we shall marry and be puzzled forever after. After all, you are only my second cousin. After closing my eyes to reread your one hundred and eighty-one words of explanation, one misspelling (so far), and Freudian question-mark at the end, I think I see what you mean by the merit of simplicity. But all the same, you are unquestionably right in your discovery that the young are all classicists, and I wish I had invented it myself. Still, we must walk before we can run, as I feel sure Professor Batchellor also used to say. Now how about putting some of your classicists to work? Here is what I wish you would do: ...

I believe you have simultaneously given the answer—I mean an answer which will serve as a frame of reference, upon which old and new data can be arranged for inspection—even a religion is that—an answer both to the Sherry problem and to the limerick problem. Now it won't be necessary for me to continue with the story I began by telling you about the baby who clammed up. Into the bargain, you have given me a useful word. I feel as happy about your 'hiding' (Please may I play with it a while?) as Costard with his remuneration; it shall be a guerdon to me. Most sweet gardon; I will do it, ma'am, in print. I hope to find another word to match it; meanwhile, I am mailing you a small token of esteem. By the way, what did you ever do about that Superintendent?

As grateful as I am for your gift, I will not tell you what I did about that Superintendent. I must keep that for my very own. As for your perfectly superb gift, you shouldn't have done it. Yet I cannot bear to give it up so I am going to keep it. I shall treasure it always and wear it only on state occasions, of which there are (is that good English?) fortunately a suitable number in the coming season when all the community is frozen and still everybody feels free to unfreeze. (I do not know if that is an English word either, but you do not seem to mind.) I spoke to Babe with respect to that. She gave me such a queer look that I felt I must explain. I reread your letters and gave her a garbled account of them. She relaxed a little then saying (I simply must tell you) that perhaps I felt too old to accept a gift of clothing from a man but a fur hat (or should it be called a cap?) is not quite a garment after all. She advised me to keep it and to send you a necktie. She called it a cravat, a word which I had never heard her use before. It makes me happy that she is not afraid to tease me, but was 'too old' really a slip of the tongue. Perhaps one reason why I still call her Babe is that, although very mature on the whole, she still has a childish way of turning things inside out to see how they will look or sound. Surely you know what I mean. It reminds me of the paper folding game in which you fold and refold and convert picture frame to two boats to a box to a smaller and better picture frame to Columbus' ship with sails which can be hoisted and lowered after all. Why did I write 'after all'? I don't know myself any more. After all! Now I must go straight out and discover a suitable necktie for you. That should not be very difficult, because you always wear white shirts, don't you? They remind me of paper, waiting to be written on. (How could I get rid of that preposition at the end?) . . . Your proposal for the rowdies is probably all right, but I wish to keep it in reserve. It will be just as good next year. I think I know more about boys than you do, you see, and I may even be right. At all events, I have begun in quite a different way. The Principal will back me up (that must make me sound like an automobile, but I do not seem to care any more) if the Superintendent hears. The boys can manage the parents. If they cannot, no one can. I first prepared them by casually informing them what a Seminar is, while doing my best to appear to be speaking of other matters. I did that one week ago. Three days from today I

am going to lay my three collections of Paul

Bunyan tales before them, and I shall ask their assistance in determining which of the stories in each book is genuine and which are made up out of whole cloth. That is, I believe they can tell me, if anyone can, which stories are spurious and probably made in New York or some other foreign place. At all events, I should learn a great deal about their literary tastes and criteria, whether they are unanimous or not. I have a strange feeling about it—that what they do will probably be a surprise to me but that it will be all right—that they will know what they are doing. I told Babe about that, and she said the queerest thing. I am not sure I dare tell you what she said. I shall do it anyway. She said that that is what looking forward to getting married feels like! Including my knowing that I am doing the right thing without knowing why. Aw, I give up! as I once overheard her saying to Stephen. Oh. No, she wouldn't do anything wrong. Moritura te saluto!

So you will not, repeat won't, tell us what you did about that Superintendent, will you not? Did you ever try not to think about hippopotamusses for one minute on a bet? I am skipping my next physical. I am afraid the doctor will say I have high blood pressure and I don't want to miss this. It's the first time since before I got married. It is true that I wore only white shirts until recently. That way, I never had to think about what color shirt to put on. But some time ago I happened to reconsider that motive, and straightway I went out and got a couple of those light blue shirts called TV shirts because they do not dazzle the iconoscope. Now it's your move. I know you save carbons of all your letters, but I'd advise you to burn the last set without rereading them. If you say you have done so, I will convert my copy into fragments and perhaps into pulp. I don't like to burn print or writing, even typewriting. You may tell me why when you can. No, it isn't because of what Babe said. I only hope Sherry is as mature when she reaches that age. No doubt it will depend on her Stephens. I am referring to the messages and styles of your whole letter, and what is hiding in them. Try repeatedly changing the punctuation, and underlining this or that word. Then go back and check the spelling in the dream story. You will probably destroy the monster before going very far. If not, write and tell me so. I may have a surprise.

I DID NOT REPEAT NOT DESTROY THOSE DARLING
LITTLE MONSTERS

Very well, Miss Frankenstein, you asked for it. What is wrong with you, my girl, is that there is a Writer inside of you, struggling to break out of the chrysalis. I will help you to help yourself. Your complaint is what used to be called being inspired, or possessed by demons. The cure is worse than the disease, and more fun. If you feel like going in for it, you can do it by yourself. But I'd like very much to help. If you will let me, meet me under the blasted oak at midnight and we will sign a contract in our commingled blood. Your first obligation is that you shall give me leave to use whatever I happen to learn from you. I promise to use it honestly. That will be easy, now. Do you see what I mean about the cure? Do that, and the fine print can wait.

PLEASE REPEAT PRETTY PLEASE I HAVE MADE MY LAST SHALL

Here is your first homework assignment. Among your papers there is a technical article which you started to write more than once, intending to freely give a considerable number of people certain information which more or less accidentally came into your possession, so that they could act more wisely after reading it. In short, you've just got to wise people up.

Got that? Check the wording; the words were all chosen deliberately, and there are quite a few separately important points in it. I counted a sweet sixteen. I counted them from your letters. You are, you see, such a complicated person that the only way you can function at all (like the centipede in the fable, disabled by an inquisitive toad) is simply to trust yourself. I am not asking you to analyse yourself; I have done it for you, and have made up a prescription to fit. Now go ahead and rummage, checklist in hand:

1) Is it technical? Don't be afraid of the word; it only means has it got a frame of reference?

2) Article? Articulate, hanging together (you prayed) once you got it finished, though not before you wrote it complete.

3) Started? Not just hoped about.

4) Write? Means wording two or more successive sentences even if only in your head (the write place).

5) More than once? Once on paper will qualify you; thereafter (not before) any skullwriting after a delay counts in your favor.

6) Intending? Not just killing time.

7) Freely give? Not sell for fee or place or power or glory or anything but love; and then

only in the sense that this is your own love: you will be glad if love is returned, but you are not dependent on that as a motive for writing.

8) Considerable number? Means worth considering: one will do, but then it must be one supposed to be out of reach otherwise than by print, something like a Personal in the London *Times,* or one who lives in a parallel universe (science fiction stuff, you know, or ask the boys) reachable only through print.

9) People? Look at yourself; for you there is no other definition; only you can recognize yourself in this mirror.

10) Certain? You are not certain at the moment, but if you ever got that article written you would be certain of what was in it; more than that, any old or new idea would be instantly recognizable to you as belonging inside or belonging outside of this article.

11) Information? Not emotion, not personalities, and so on, but simply a pattern of points in some sort of relation to each other and to the center of the universe; you will of course present the information only by stating the relations, leaving the points to take care of themselves at least for the present; you may say that you could write only about persons

and emotions, but for the present you must trust me and the fine print will take care of itself; see also 'frame of reference' and 'people' above; or in other words, personality minus identity leaves information.

12) More or less accidentally? Some accident was in it, you feel, and never mind how much or little; this makes you humble; you are incapable of being proud of discovering something, but you are always proud of passing the dope on; and when you tell people how you found out, that is only more information to make them wise enough to do it too.

13) Came into your possession? If you had been elsewhere you most likely never would have been handed this hot potato; now that it is in your custody you simply must pass it on or it will explode.

14) Act? Not simply feel, but Do Something; then the other people around them (you can't seem to focus on those others) can just feel as far as you are concerned; they are too blurred and far away to matter, and what is biting you now is that your readers must act, as they then see fit, of course, because you trust them vastly more than you trust yourself to act, after all.

15) More wisely? You don't know how to feel wise yourself, but your twins (see 'people') will be, once they get this information from you, so wondrous wise that the world will be an utterly different place, and you can't help hoping that you will live to see it then (though that hope feels selfish).

16) After reading it? You have a sense of Time, you see, also spelled CONSCIENCE; when you neglect to publish your hot potato in time, you give yourself a headache for a punishment; if you ever feel vaguely and generally guilty about any matters at all, then, to gain the suitable punishment for that vague guilty feeling you proceed to neglect your publishing and the rest is automatic; since you have not yet published notably in print, you have so far published by formal discourse, also spelled TEACHING; now this is not enough for you, since you don't trust yourself to think cleverly enough on your feet to earn your pay; yet you have whipped yourself on for years and now do your formal discourse facilely enough to awe the multitude and satisfy almost anybody but yourself.

There you are; now find that draft.

I HAVE FOUND TWO NOW WHAT DO I DO NEXT

TWO IS FINE SINCE THEY MULTIPLY LIKE RABBITS
  LETTER FOLLOWS

Toss coin to choose. Paraphrase to fit typed
lines exactly 60 units long. No fudging: standard spacing everywhere, no word broken by
hyphen unless hyphen anyhow. Oh. Well, some
day you might read a few pages of *Time* maga-
zine, and my Lora letters, to hear what hyphens
sound like. Don't think now; just reword, meanwhile concentrating your so-called mind upon
mechanics of page in typewriter, striving only
to make machine do thinking for you. One to
two hundred words will do, take an hour or so.
Find yourself changing original message somewhat, don't worry: only an exercise. Use Roget
Thesaurus to taste, but never a dictionary.
When done, take out of oven and re-do 59
wide; then 58, 57, 56, etc., until suddenly
enough (like Chinese dinner). So doing, let
paragraph rearrange itself, reject any message
it likes and offer you others. First two or three
versions worse and worse, then over the hump
and coasting down; stop before reaching Slough
of Despond. Then do the same with chunk of
other article. Shuffle all versions together and
spread out. Stand there, white-shirted type-

writer impatiently waiting for you, surveying until you can't stand it any longer. Probably about forty seconds. You are thinking of your twins in mortal danger, uninformedly living along on their parallel world which is going to collapse at any moment; you've got to get your saving message to them before the last print leaves; you don't know yet what the message will be, but you attack the typewriter with both fists and spatter the one and only message all over the white shirt-front.

Don't send me anything of this; I won't look at it. Done? Take a deep breath and write to tell me what it felt like. Or write a sonnet.

It was a horrifying experience, I'm here to tell you, cousin, but I'm here for all that. In very truth, more here than ever—there is more here inside of me than before I started batting it out (old bat from Battyville, they call me, Slugger) and I'm more at home here than a home-maker. How long has this been going on, for weeping bitterly into the soup? And how much longer, you old tandem you? If this is what getting married feels like, I understand Tomcat Mandeville and what's-all-her-names both now, and they deserve to marry each other. Serves me right. Come out from behind that moustache, you old Skeezicks: now I know who I have sold my soul to and where to tell you to go to and D the prepositions. Oh, Shaw.

You needn't have been quite so concerned about item number eleven, 'Information.' I checked it by items 9, 10, 13, and 15, and immediately found myself thinking simultaneously of the police classification-system for finger-prints and of Goethe's 'Elective Affinities.' . . .

DONT REPEAT DONT LOOK AT CARBON BEFORE GETTING MY LETTER

Your report does not call the work a 'headache,' I see. Now listen carefully. Without a glance at the text, take the carbon of the first sheet, together with a clean envelope and a razor-blade, to a very bright eight-year-old girl who can be trusted to keep a secret and not cut herself. Hand her the carbon and warn her not to read it aloud to you. In the exact center of the first paragraph, she is to find the word 'soup' with question-mark. The next sentence also ends with a question-mark; these are the only two in the letter. She is to cut out the second question sentence and put it in the envelope for you. Now you can start thinking if you like. Never tell me; confide in Babe if you like, she can tell Stephen, and Stephen will tell me only what he thinks I ought to know, which will probably be nothing. Real men never talk about women except in generalities; the individuals are too important.

Your first paragraph compares illuminatingly with your earlier letters—the ones with all the darling little monsters. Here there is nothing of the sort at all—no confusion in the ambiguities, rather multiple depth all readable down to rock bottom. Down there, no snake-pit. Even the final pun was frankly advertised. If you had written 'pshaw,' I would have recognized him behind the plumage but probably not you; this way, he can't bite either of us. Agenbite of inwit. Now I can start breathing again.

About the personality-profiles now. (You didn't think I wouldn't recognize them? I can even make a stab at what you did about that Superintendent. Hippopotamusses!) A word of friendly advice from an old hand. Don't try too hard to humanize the mathematics directly, by brute force. You are going to calculate, and you are going to write a warm human article, but don't mix the two. I mean, don't try very hard to. They will mix themselves if there is adequate affinity. If that doesn't happen by itself, you will know that you have only discovered America instead of reaching India. Do the mathematics first. The work may last for months or years; but suddenly, some day, the mathematics will shout: 'Look, mama! No hands!' Then it is done. Because you did it all yourself, you can't lose it any more.

Now you are ready to humanize. The wrong way, which you must not try to carry through, will be described first. I do this first for a reason which a little story will make clear. I protected Sherry, or rather showed her how to protect herself, against ever pinching her fingers dangerously, when she was very small. I don't remember exactly when, but I know it was between twelve and twenty-two months because I can see the kitchen where we did it. I showed her how I could hurt myself in closing a drawer which I could see she wanted to close and could. She observed my pain with interest, then very accurately measured out a dose of the same pain for herself. She showed me her fingers to check; I saw that there was no damage whatever and that the pain would fade in a minute or so. It was enough. She evidently had had enough pain, never hurt herself that way again. Visitors would start and tremble at the sight; Sherry would open and close all sorts of things with amazing dexterity, her fingers slipping out of the way a hair's-breadth before disaster. Some months later I showed her how I could hurt her hand in the hinge side of a door that I was closing, to teach her that pain could come from other persons too; she said she knew that already and needed no test with her own hand. Then I began to fear that I had made a mistake. Probably it was one; there have been evidences of it. Too clever by half. But you are mature, and know better than to believe something because you see it in print or typing.

Well, as I see it, the wrong way is to start at the beginning of your mathematics and proceed to convert it, in logical sequence, into expository prose, trying to humanize more or less as you go and expecting to finish that in the revisions. It won't work. That is not what the exercises have been getting you ready for. All during the mathematics, the exercises were continuing, but at very low pressure. That is important. Don't strain yourself. Probably a good bet would be the contents of the high-school weekly: without the striving for perfection, it can be a better game than card-solitaire, very likely better than Scrabble, which however is better for sociability. Let kids catch you at it; don't force your product or your methods on them; don't supervise their attempts, but praise every result whatever: young people criticize themselves too much anyhow. When this gets boring, reverse the scale and write a sonnet.

All this while, the people behind the mathematics have been bottled up like jinn in metal bottles. But now the mathematics is done and laid away, and like children bursting out of school here they come running. You will be overwhelmed by the confusion, but gradually you will sort it out to make them happiest. How? Could you give me the rules for managing a picnic? Oh, yes; that Superintendent has mimeographed rules for you, but did they ever work? Nothing works but an alert affectionate eye.

Suddenly you can do no more. Don't try: that way lies the Slough of Despond. Lay it all away, and leave it untouched for from three to ten days. Take it out again, but this time—and it is the first time—you consider the over-all plan. Your picnic is too well organized; shuffle the groups, break them up and recombine them into different groups. Take it from there—it's your picnic. Just don't try to make it perfect; quit before the people rebel; print it so.

I had almost forgotten that you did a German minor; now I see you with unerring instinct turning to the Wahlverwandtschaften, the most feminine of Goethe's longer works. I don't mean the wording—any phonograph can listen —I mean the values, the motives and their balancing. Iphigenia, on the other hand, feels strongly masculine to me, Tasso between. You don't have to agree with me. Then, remembering your medieval interests, let me just mumble that Kudrun seems to have been composed by a woman with only a theoretical knowledge of men, but the Nibelungenlied by a man with an intimate knowledge of women. Our traditions favor that sort of unbalance; I don't think it's biological, the mutilated and missing chromosomes and all that, though there is certainly the difference that women are tougher than men, less distressed by foul odors and so on— you have read Spurgeon on Shakespeare's imagery of course, so you have the mathematics

for that. Goethe, on the other hand, had none
—one of the few things he lacked. Look at his
prescientific writings, their god-like fumbling
with shades and hues of color, and those arche-
types! Chemistry. Girls love the elective affinities in it; but they generally want to make only
stable compounds, can't bear instability. How
can you get progress that way? Or don't you
want it? I know there is a good deal of the
feminine in me; how much of the masculine is
there in you? Will you settle for dynamic stability, a structure continuing to cohere only because it is always changing?

I carried the first sheet of your letter and the
first sheet, folded shut, of my carbon to Eleanor.
(I don't call her out of her name any more, and
I know why.) She is after all the brightest eight-
year-old available on short notice, when adequately stimulated to be. Solemn as such a child
ought to be, she got as far as slipping the piece
out of sight in the envelope; then jerked it out
again so hurriedly that she tore the envelope.
Took one glance, then gave me a look which
gradually and swiftly warmed up to where we
were exactly the same age. She said she wouldn't
tell Stephen anything, that he knows too much
already. Us women have got to stick together,

she said, or we get stuck separately. And yet she trusts Stephen, you know: it was the principle of the thing. As for you, you of course know too much too, but she will trust you if I do. There. That's all you get told. I found her grammar very accurate, as an eight-year-old's grammar ought to be.

I am going to be moderately busy for a while, but will be sending notes to your wife.

I am keeping no carbon of this, and you won't show it to me; this is the contractual equivalent of burning it. You see: I can't help it if my fine print is not the same as yours. Looking over your last letter again, I see that I ought to have answered your question about headaches before. What's a 'headache?' I've never had one in my life. Otherwise, things are normal here. But now some snippets:

There are not only two sexes, and perhaps other dichotomies, but there are also two sects of fully (childishly) humans. One sect plays with literature, the other with science. They have got to get together to propagate the community of the future. One for one. Not hard to do, because they are indistinguishable then: they go to different churches, get equivalently exalted. Proselytizing? Hands off. No hands. Two mechanisms, interchangeable parts.

Why not just tell the inside story? Answer: A writer is never more honest than in his myths: he knows better than to trust plain memory. Must condense. Take it apart, fold it smaller. And deeper. Reminds me of something, will remind reader. Doesn't have to be the same thing; looks for still more, still deeper. Does the better part herself. Better half. Hiding. Us women.

Two mechanisms. Different races? Nonsense. Lived together for so long, handwriting looks alike, that's all. Different enough to make it interesting. Shaw and John Bull. We need the Irish. They have the power. The giftie gie us. Not even a sparrow. What is truth? Would not stay to answer tomorrow. Cruel and unusual laughter. Constitution. Nine men, getting younger all the time. Fast enough? Dynamic stability. Have to run hard as can stay in one place. The French just tear theirs up, start again from mathematics. Children starve meanwhile. Do something.

I got bored with sonnets and high-school news both, so dug up a synopsis of Wolfram's

Parzival that I made when I was doing Middle High German. Sure enough, there was a part which exactly fits my problem, though I don't know which is Gawan, Sigune, Parzival, or Trevrizent. Or the horse. I believe you would rather be the horse than Trevrizent, and I am sure you are not Sigune. Are you writing or Doing Something? What she did was about as negative as you can get. You are not sophomoric enough to be Gawan, that perfect gentle knight. It is plain to see why chivalry had to vanish: no dynamic stability in it. Self-satisfaction is death; the Second Law of Thermodynamics says so. Let us, then, both be Parzival; for at least he stuck out his neck, like the turtle, without which he can't go anywhere. We'll take turns, MWF and TTS, and visit Trevrizent on Sunday, for so it is written in the constitution. And we do respect the judge more than the soldier; fortunately for the present they are both interested in baseball. Be that as it may, since I am not Doing Something I have rewritten this piece of the synopsis as an exercise:

Leaving Parzival's adventures unreported, Wolfram follows the extremely complicated adventures of Gawan, while Parzival shows up at times in the background, so that we can learn how he is defeating knights and requiring his prisoners to try to get the Holy Grail for him. We next meet Parzival at the hermitage where Sigune keeps watch over the grave of her lover. She forgives him for his mistake at Munsalvaesche, and advises him to follow Kundrie, who brings Sigune food from the Grail each week, and who has just now left her. Parzival loses track of Kundrie. He fights and defeats a Knight of the Grail, and rides further on the man's horse, because his own was lost in the fight. Presently he meets a knight who is making a pilgrimage -- to the hermit Trevrizent, in fact; this knight reproves Parzival for riding armed on Good Friday, and advises him to go see Trevrizent. Now Parzival for the very first time turns to God in his thoughts, and says to himself, 'What if God can undo my woe? If today is his day of help (remembering that this is Good Friday), let him help me if he can.' Now he puts God to the test: deliberately he gets off the proper road to Trevrizent and then gives the horse its head, to see what God's guidance and control of living beings will amount to. The test succeeds.

That is Progress, believe it or not. I am working on something printable, yes. The only thing wrong with it, in principle, is that so far it has no beginning. The end will take care of itself, exactly the opposite of what most composition students will say of them. Their trouble is that they haven't done the mathematics first, so they have very little to say. The closed system will take care of the end, but offers no beginning. The beginning has got to be human. A surface value, if you like: a nugget lying on the surface to attract the miners. What I need is something like that, anything at all which bears a resemblance to the inside message. Resemblance, not identity. Some little pattern in the mathematical model must also be a symbol of a real-world item so familiar to the reader that he simply must stop, look & listen. When I find it I won't feel tired any more.

I believe I have found what I need to start me off, just as you need a beginning. You can use it if you will, and I don't mean 'may.' It's in the contract, isn't it? You have the right to use it, therefore I have no right to give you permission. Your project surely has a dichotomy in it somewhere; mine, as you know, is the two sects, science and literature. It is clear to me, right now, which one is ahead. But of course, while the text rewrites itself with me listening, the other may slide past and come out ahead after all. I'm not going to impose my preconceived ideas on a text in English, the language I love; it shall speak, and I will listen. Vox populi vox dei. I'm only an editor. Is that what you were hoping I would turn out to be? I wouldn't put it past you. Well, here it is:

A certain railroad station in Ireland has two clocks which disagree by several minutes. When a helpful English traveler pointed out the fact to a porter, the reply was, 'Faith, sir, if they told the same time, why should there be two of them?'